MONGOL WARRIORS

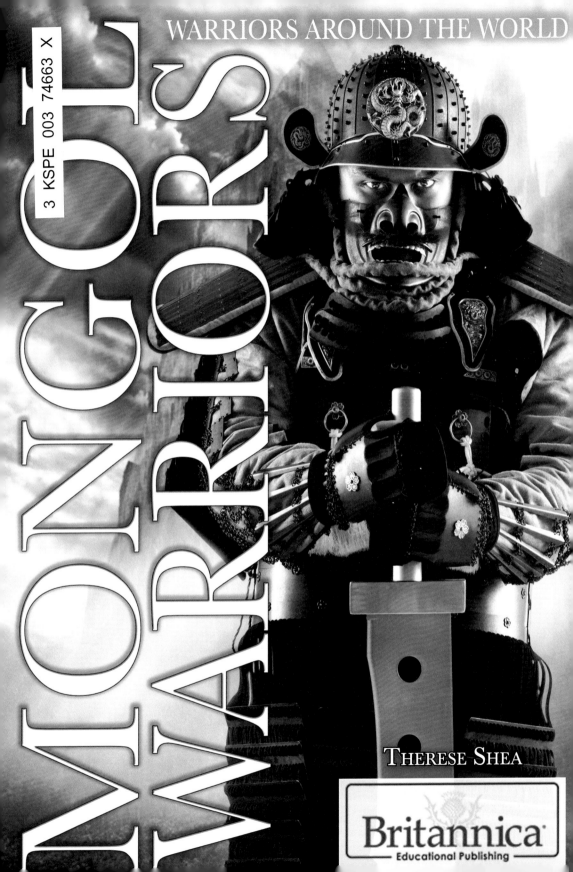

MONGOL WARRIORS

THERESE SHEA

Britannica
Educational Publishing

Published in 2017 by Britannica Educational Publishing (a trademark of Encyclopædia Britannica, Inc.) in association with The Rosen Publishing Group, Inc.
29 East 21st Street, New York, NY 10010

Distributed exclusively by Rosen Publishing.
To see additional Britannica Educational Publishing titles, go to rosenpublishing.com.

First Edition

Britannica Educational Publishing
J.E. Luebering: Executive Director, Core Editorial
Anthony L. Green: Editor, Compton's by Britannica

Rosen Publishing
Carolyn DeCarlo: Editor
Nelson Sá: Creative Director
Matt Cauli: Designer
Cindy Reiman: Photography Manager
Nicole Reinholdt: Photo Researcher

Library of Congress Cataloguing-in-Publication Data

Names: Shea, Therese, author.
Title: Mongol warriors / Therese Shea.
Description: First edition. | New York, NY : Britannica Educational Publishing, in association with Rosen Educational Services, 2017. | Series: Warriors around the world | Audience: Grades 5 to 8. | Includes bibliographical references and index.
Identifiers: LCCN 2016020473| ISBN 9781508103752 (library bound) | ISBN 9781508104353 (pbk) | ISBN 9781508103011 (6-pack)
Subjects: LCSH: Mongols–History–Juvenile literature. | Mongols–Warfare–Juvenile literature. | Military art and science–Mongolia–History–To 1500–Juvenile literature.
Classification: LCC DS19 .S518 2016 | DDC 950/.2–dc23
LC record available at https://lccn.loc.gov/2016020473

Manufactured in China

Photo credits: Cover, p. 3 Blend Images/Colin Anderson/Getty Images; p. 7 Wolfgang Kaehler/LightRocket/Getty Images; pp. 8–9, 33, 42 Encyclopaedia Britannica, Inc.; pp. 10, 24 DEA/M. Seemuller/De Agostini/Getty Images; pp. 12–13 flocu/Shutterstock.com; p. 14 (inset) Hugh Sitton/Corbis Documentary/Getty Images; p. 15 David Edwards/National Geographic Image Collection/Getty Images; pp. 16–17 Courtesy of the Edinburgh University Library, Scotland; pp. 20–21 Strelyuk/Shutterstock.com; p. 23 LandscaperY/Shutterstock.com; p. 27 DEA/A. Dagli Orti/De Agostini/Getty Images; pp. 28–29, 32, 35 Pictures from History/Bridgeman Images; p. 31 Fosco Maraini/Monkmeyer; p. 36 University of Texas Libraries; p. 37 (inset) © North Wind Picture Archives/Alamy Stock Photo; p. 38 Russian Academy of Sciences Library Depository St. Petersburg/Sputnik/Bridgeman Images; p. 40 Courtesy of the National Palace Museum, Taipei, Taiwan, Republic of China; interior pages border images © iStockphoto.com/Rawpixel Ltd (warrior with outstretched arm), © iStockphoto.com/joyt (landscape with yurts), © iStockphoto.com/ Enkhtamir Enkhdavaa (mounted warrior); pp. 14, 22, 25, 30, 32, 37 (background) ©iStockphoto.com/RPBMedia.

CONTENTS

INTRODUCTION

T he Central Asian people known as the Mongols occupy a vast highland region called the steppe in what is now Mongolia and the Inner Mongolia Autonomous Region of China. The Mongols share a common language and a tradition of following a nomadic way of life herding livestock. The Mongols' origin is a mystery, but their place in medieval history is unforgettable. They announced their existence—by force—across the continents of Europe and Asia beginning in the 1200s CE.

A thirteenth-century English monk named Matthew Paris called the Mongols a "detestable nation of Satan that poured out like devils from Tartarus [hell]." How did a pastoral people create such hostility? Life on the steppe was far from peaceful. In fact, it was a bit like constantly being in battle.

In the thirteenth century, an alliance of nomadic Mongol tribes became a powerful military force. Under the leadership of Genghis Khan and his successors, they established an empire that reached from what are now China and Korea in the east to Eastern Europe and the shores of the Persian Gulf in the west. At the height of their power, the Mongols overthrew the rulers of northern and southern China and reunited China under Mongol rule. Though the influence of the Mongol Empire declined greatly in the fourteenth century, the Mongols are still remembered today for their unprecedented military success, owed partly to their unusual lifestyle.

Much of Mongolia today still looks as it did in the thirteenth century when the Mongols rose to power across the continent.

A Mongol warrior did not join the army but, rather, was born into it. Every Mongol man who could ride a horse was a soldier, and all became expert equestrians early in life. The Mongol prowess for riding was especially noticed in collaboration with their

The Mongol Empire grew to encompass many cultures across Europe and Asia far different than its own.

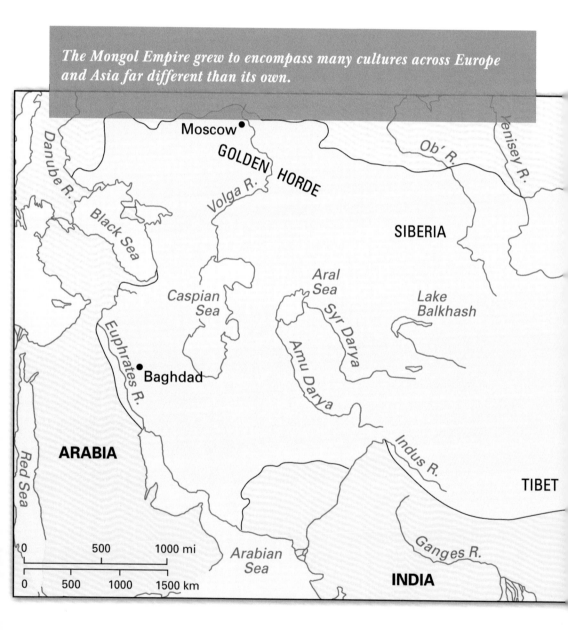

skill as archers on moving horses. The Mongol warrior was always ready to fight, whether he was hunting wild animals or going to war. He met both challenges with vigor and an eagerness to prove his courage and fighting expertise.

The Mongols were not always the army with the best weapons, the strongest armor, or the largest forces, yet they were often the victors. Unparalleled ferocity, dazzling battlefield tactics, and brilliant leadership were common factors in their successes. Extraordinary discipline was also an essential component; in fact, desertion meant death.

Though the Mongols did not adopt a written language until Genghis Khan's reign, a significant work of their early literature—*Mongqolun niuča tobča'an* (*Secret History of the Mongols*)—survives to relate the details of the Mongols' rise. It is a chronicle of the deeds of Genghis Khan and of his son Ögödei, composed no earlier

A COMPTON'S MAP

Lake Baikal

Amur R.

Karakorum

NGOLIA

KOREA

Peking

Yellow Sea

CHINA

Yangtze R.

East China Sea

South China Sea

9

كشيده بنداوان كرد دود وخلى كسه وسركشه شوند ونوروز مهم كسف ولشكران طرف بروز امد

An ancient Mongolian saying is "A Mongol without a horse is like a bird without the wings." This Persian manuscript reflects the Mongols' extraordinary horsemanship, even in battle.

than 1228, that was written at least partly to praise the leaders but also to record that era of history. Other than this, almost all writers, even those who were in the Mongol service, dwelt on tales of Mongol invasions and the destruction that resulted from it. All these sources reveal information about the thrilling ascent of the Mongol warrior, one of the most intriguing tales of the medieval world.

CHAPTER 1
MYSTERIOUS, MENACING MONGOLS

The first mention of peoples who can be identified with Mongolia can be found in Chinese accounts from around 2000 BCE. However, the first inhabitants of whom there is certainty are the Xiongnu, who were recorded to have lived there by about the fifth or fourth century BCE. The Xiongnu are thought by modern Mongols to be their remote ancestors.

A NOMADIC PEOPLE

The Mongols were pastoralists who were superb horsemen and traveled with flocks of sheep, goats, cattle, and horses over the immense grasslands of Central Asia. The nomadic Mongols moved seasonally, bringing livestock and entire camps from one pasture to another. They lived in portable dwellings called *gers* (or *yurts*), which were erected on wooden poles and covered with skin, felt, or hand-woven textiles in bright colors. The *ger* was carried from place to place on horseback or by wagon.

Mongols traveled with their food and clothing sources as well. Their livestock provided milk, meat, and wool, which was used to make felt. They wore heavy coats lined with fur and boots made of felt and leather. The Mongols also hunted and ate wild game, and, in especially hard circumstances, drank the blood of their horses.

A primary advantage of a ger is that it is easily transported, an asset that remains in the dwellings of today. Gers of the legendary Mongol warriors would have looked similar to this.

WHERE ARE THEY NOW?

Today, Mongols form the bulk of the population of independent Mongolia, and they comprise about one-sixth of the population of the Inner Mongolia Autonomous Region of China. Elsewhere in China are communities of Mongols in Qinghai province and the autonomous regions of Xinjiang and Tibet and in the Northeast (Manchuria and the Liaoning, Jilin, and Heilongjiang provinces). There are also groups in Russia's Siberia. All these populations speak dialects of the Mongol language, and many retain aspects of their historical customs.

Many Mongolian children continue to be raised in the traditional nomadic, herding lifestyle of their ancestors.

With a few exceptions, Mongol social structure, economy, and language changed very little over many centuries. Traditional Mongol society was based on the family. Several families made up a clan, and clans combined to form tribes. In the tribe, weaker clans retained their own leaders, but were subordinate to the strongest clan.

The head of the tribe was called the khan. He had the authority to order migrations, assign lands for livestock, and make other leadership decisions. He was assisted with decision-making

Shamanism is still present in the Mongolian culture. Here, a Mongolian shaman performs a ritual, serving as a link between the human world and the world of spirits.

by the tribal shaman, an individual believed to be connected to the spiritual world. A khan was only in power as long as his people believed in his leadership, usually demonstrated through his ability to bring them to good pasture and provide riches through victorious battle campaigns.

HERDSMAN AND SOLDIER

In daily Mongol life, raiding to capture livestock, women, and prisoners was a recognized method of gaining property. And Mongols did not just fight Mongols. Other peoples on the steppe included the Tatars, the Merkits, and the Khitan. Every Mongol who could ride and bear arms was both a herdsman and a soldier according to the need of the moment. There was no such thing as a civilian. Many chronicles tell of Mongol women taking part in battles, too.

Because Mongols fought on horseback, their weapons were usually designed to be used while riding. The most prized was the bow. Mongol warriors might take up to a year making a bow and usu-

ally carried two or even three into battle. Though small, their bows had a range of up to 300 yards (275 meters).

A warrior carried as many as sixty arrows. Different kinds of arrows were used for different situations. Some were best for long distances. Others were suitable for piercing armor or injecting poison into a victim. Still more arrows were lit on fire to scare enemies. Mongols also used hollow arrows that made a whistling sound for signaling during deafening combat.

This miniature painting of Mongol warriors ready for battle was created for an Islamic history book from 1307 called History of the World.

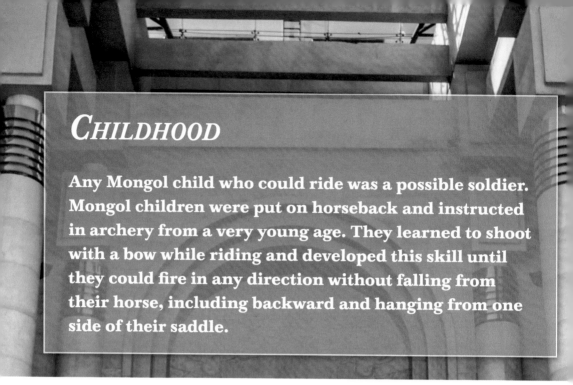

CHILDHOOD

Any Mongol child who could ride was a possible soldier. Mongol children were put on horseback and instructed in archery from a very young age. They learned to shoot with a bow while riding and developed this skill until they could fire in any direction without falling from their horse, including backward and hanging from one side of their saddle.

Mongol leather armor protected both the warrior and his horse. Later in the empire, many soldiers wore iron scales or chain mail. Silk undershirts were worn to protect the body, too. Helmets of iron or steel were a conical shape. Mongols also carried lances, maces, daggers, and curved swords called sabers. A Mongol warrior cared for his own weapons, equipment, food, and up to five extra horses. Discipline in caring for these items was imperative: even commanding officers could be punished for ill-equipped soldiers.

In the Mongol culture, a form of hunting called the *nerge* served as entertainment, a way to acquire meat for winter, and a practice that kept warriors ready for battle. Everyone participated in the months-long activity. Warriors worked in teams across the vast steppe, communicating with each other through messengers, flag waving, and torch burning. The teams closed in, eventually trapping animals in a ring, making them easier to kill. The Mongols then demonstrated combat skills for their khan with swords, knives, and other weapons both on horseback and on foot. Many aspects of the nerge were translated into battlefield tactics, aiding Mongol factions in surrounding their enemy.

This was the warrior culture into which the infamous Genghis Khan was born and rose to power. He harnessed the skills of his people, uniting tribes and assembling an army that would go down in history as one of the most terrifying of all time.

19

CHAPTER 2
GENGHIS KHAN: WARRIOR KING

Mongol history alternated between periods of tribal conflict and tribal consolidation. It was the infamous Mongol warrior-king Genghis Khan who united the tribes most successfully to conquer the steppe and the lands and peoples beyond. Many of the legends illustrating the Mongol warriors' fierceness originated during his rule. And much of what we know of Genghis Khan's life is legendary, as described in the embellished *Secret History of the Mongols*.

What is certain is the great leader was born sometime between 1155 and 1167. He was named Temüjin (or Temuchin). When he was nine, his father Yesügei, a member of the royal Borjigin clan of the Mongols, was poisoned by a band of Tatars. With Yesügei dead, the remainder of the clan, led by the rival Taychiut family, abandoned his widow, Höelün, and her children.

TEMÜJIN'S REVENGE

For a time, Temüjin's family led a life of extreme poverty. However, they preserved some power as

members of the royal Borjigin clan. Temüjin was able to claim the wife whom Yesügei had selected for him just before his death. But the Merkit people, a tribe living in northern Mongolia, bore Temüjin a grudge because Yesügei had stolen his wife Höelün from one of them. In turn, they stole Temüjin's wife, a woman named Börte.

This steel-covered statue of Genghis Khan is more than 130 feet (40 meters) tall. It is located east of the Mongolian capital of Ulaanbaatar.

Temüjin appealed to the khan of the Kereit tribe, Toghril, to help him. Toghril was at that time the most powerful Mongol leader. Toghril and Temüjin's father had shared the relationship of *andas*. Out of respect for that bond, Toghril furnished Temüjin with 20,000 soldiers and persuaded Jamuka, Temüjin's boyhood friend, to supply an army as well. With such forces behind him, Temüjin easily overpowered the Merkit.

Not long after, Temüjin treated the nobility of the Jürkin clan in the same way. These princes, supposedly his allies, had plundered his property. In revenge, Temüjin eliminated the Jürkin nobles and took the common people as his own soldiers and servants. When his power had grown sufficiently for him to risk a final showdown with the formidable Tatars, he defeated them in battle and slaughtered all except

THE TALES OF TEMÜJIN

Several stories illustrate Temüjin's power of attracting supporters through sheer force of personality, even as a young man. In one, he was captured by the Taychiut, who, rather than killing him, kept him around their camps, wearing a wooden collar. One night, when they were feasting, Temüjin knocked down the sentry with a blow and fled. The Taychiut searched all night for him. Finally, he was seen by one of their people, who, impressed by the fire in his eyes, helped him escape at the risk of his own life.

the youngest children. The Tatar children would grow to become loyal followers of the Mongols.

UNIFICATION AND CONSOLIDATION

At last, the alliance with Toghril broke down, and Temüjin dispersed his people, the Kereits, among the Mongols as servants and troops as well. This ruthlessness was not mere cruelty, it was strategy. Temüjin intended to leave alive none of the old rival leaders, who might prove a focus of resistance; to provide himself with a fighting force; and, above all, to crush the sense of clan loyalties and to unite all the nomads in personal obedience to his family.

Hansaray, also called the Khan's Palace, is located in the town of Bakhchysarai in Crimea. Built in the sixteenth century, it became home to a number of khans who succeeded Genghis Khan.

وبرتت اوبحل ومروق اذشاه
جبرشداین وسماه محری درآنم درا وابدضلهاد جنیکرجان وبه دانونی نداته سیدبای کردبدکعبی باعطت زبائدسوانق
نوربفای نرل ساخت ودران نوربغای لبب نزرک جنیکرخا ن نروی مرز کردند وساری کی بکحنبشت

A sixteenth-century Persian manuscript reveals the powerful Genghis Khan at court surrounded by soldiers and subjects.

BLOOD BROTHERS

Mongols formed bonds of loyalty with people outside their family called blood brothers, or *andas*. Each potential anda pricked a finger and mixed blood to forge the bond. Some historians say the bond called for andas to have even more loyalty to each other than biological family members. The anda relationship was essential in Genghis Khan's rise to power.

Finally, in 1206, a great assembly was held by the River Onon, and Temüjin was proclaimed Genghis Khan, a title that probably meant "Universal Ruler." Unsurprisingly for a monarch with such a title, he was not content to rule just the steppe. He soon looked to the lands outside.

The supreme khan, while prizing the Mongols' nomadic lifestyle, appreciated the advantages of settled cultures, namely the goods and riches they could offer. The first territory outside the steppe that he set his sights on was China. According to the *Secret History of the Mongols*, his army numbered over 100,000 at this time.

Chapter 3
Mongol Military Campaigns

Though the Mongols were already capable soldiers by the time Genghis Khan came to power, he and his generals can be credited for organizing and employing them effectively. Under the new system, troops were structured based on units of 10, 100, 1,000, and 10,000. Though these units often traveled apart, they attacked as a unified body.

Battle Tactics

Mongol armies on horseback could move much more quickly than those on foot, so they used that swiftness to attack their enemies quickly, before reinforcements could arrive. Coordinated attacks included ambush, hit-and-run, and wave attacks. Changes in tactics were made possible by a communication system that included riders and a system of relay stations to pass messages between leaders and those on the battlefront.

The most common battle formation was as follows: Five units of one hundred men (a *jaguns*) marched forward separately. Two jaguns were heavy cavalry, carrying maces, lances, and swords, and protected by heavy armor. Three jaguns were light cavalry, equipped with lighter armor, javelins, and bows and arrows. First, the light-cavalry jaguns advanced in silence, using flag signals to communicate orders

كورد نوفا براستان دواند وجلدرا مسروكه و بادشاه اسلام ازوادي امن اوازي بشنداكه لاتخفيوت من القوم الظلمير
وبدان ساى فوى...كدان ابسار...تار...كرنده وارون جانت باس...حل بود عاقبه الامر مصران بنكسيه سه...

The ferocity of the armies of the Mongol khans became legendary. A Persian manuscript depicts a battle between Mongolians and Egyptians in the fourteenth century.

and to attack. As they pelted the enemy with arrows and javelins, they were maneuvering to encircle them, reminiscent of the nerge hunt. Then they would withdraw to allow the heavy cavalry to attack. A deafening roar would erupt from the warriors, and war drums would begin beating. The enveloping Mongols would have their enemies nearly surrounded by then. They did not worry about completely destroying them, sometimes allowing their adversaries to slip away to spread the news of destruction.

Heavily armored Mongol warriors wore suits of small rectangular plates, or scales, of leather called lamellar armor.

Another Mongol strategy was the feigned retreat, in which Genghis's troops pretended to leave in defeat. Meanwhile, they would spread out. Their enemies would pursue them, usually in smaller, unorganized forces. When a signal was given, the "fleeing" Mongols would turn and surround the enemy. Franciscan friar Giovanni Da Pian Del Carpini reported on this maneuver: "Even if the [Mongols] retreat our men ought not to separate from each other or be split up, for the [Mongols] pretend to withdraw in order to divide an enemy."

Sometimes, the Mongol army forced prisoners to march at the front of their formation so that enemy forces would be less likely to attack—or at least fewer Mongols would be killed if they were. The captives acted as a sort of human shield.

As savage as they could be, Mongol attacks were well planned. Months before an attack, Mongol spy networks mapped routes, observed supply sources, and recorded information about defenses. The Mongols also used psychological warfare before an attack. Their spies spread misinformation among their enemies, hoping to increase their fear and make them more likely to surrender. Cities that surrendered immediately were often left intact. Those that did not could expect little mercy.

29

BUILDING AN EMPIRE

In 1211, Genghis Khan began a campaign against the Tangut kingdom of Xixia, a northwestern border state of China. After a series of raids and demonstrations of the Mongols' considerable forces, the Tangut agreed to fall under Mongol rule and pay tribute to the khan. This was a demand of all conquered territories, which also had to provide servants and additional soldiers.

In 1215, against the Jin empire of northern China, Genghis Khan sought to take the city of Zhongdu (Beijing). However, its 40-foot (12-meter) walls protected Zhongdu from normal Mongol steppe warfare. When attacking walled cities, the Mongols exercised new strategies that had been developed by the Chinese, Persians, and Arabs. Siege weapons included catapults to hurl stones, diseased animals, and flaming objects over walls. Mongols lit unneeded campfires and even made straw soldiers so that their armies would seem more numerous. In the case of Zhongdu, the

GHENGIS KHAN'S BODYGUARDS

Genghis Khan established an elite force of Mongol warriors called the *keshig*. Numbering about 10,000 in 1206, they functioned as his bodyguards. However, membership was also a way to honor the fiercest and most loyal soldiers. Keshig troops held more power than army commanders. They were also responsible for training the rest of the army.

These massive walls in the Tibet Autonomous Region were constructed of stone, brick, and mud to defend inhabitants from Mongol attacks.

Mongols surrounded the city, cutting off supply routes, until the starving people surrendered. Then he ordered the city sacked, and the Jin massacred. Once Mongol forces found their way into cities, they left them in ruins.

Next, the khan led a conquest into Khwārezm (present-day Iran). He sought revenge for the murder of an ambassador he had sent to the Khwārezm shah, the ruler of the kingdom.

Much of Genghis Khan's success in the west can be attributed to the military strategies of Mongol general Sübeedei.

NOYAN SÜBEEDEI

Sübeedei was a *noyan*, or "general," under Genghis Khan. He is remembered as a master tactician, having orchestrated some of the most impressive victories. The son of a blacksmith, he allied with Genghis Khan around 1190. He became a commander of a *tümen* (a unit of ten thousand soldiers) during the wars against the Xixia. He then led a bloody march into Iran, following the fleeing shah of Khwārezm, and then into Russia.

This was a terrible crime in the Mongol culture. It was in this war that the Mongols earned their reputation for savagery and terror. Though the Mongols were greatly outnumbered, they conquered city after city. Fields and gardens were laid waste and irrigation works destroyed. The city of Urgench was flooded when the Mongol army rerouted a nearby river. In Nishapur, it was said that even dogs and cats were killed.

The invasion of Russia was led by the noyan Sübeedei. At the 1223 battle of Kalka River (in present-day Ukraine), he and noyan Jebe defeated a combined force of Turk and Russian peoples, using a feigned retreat. It was said that the Russian generals were bound and placed under a heavy wooden platform. They suffocated as the Mongols celebrated their victory.

The Mongol Empire was spread over a vast territory, extending farther even after the death of the great Genghis Khan.

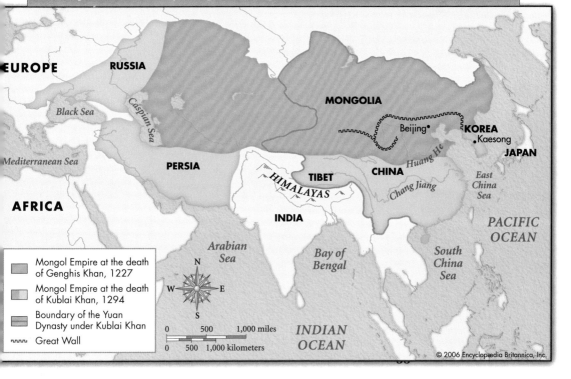

Mongol Empire at the death of Genghis Khan, 1227

Mongol Empire at the death of Kublai Khan, 1294

Boundary of the Yuan Dynasty under Kublai Khan

Great Wall

© 2006 Encyclopædia Britannica, Inc.

Genghis Khan himself did not lead his armies into war again until a final campaign against Xixia in 1226–1227. He died on August 18, 1227, after a fall from a horse. At the time of his death, his warriors had conquered the landmass extending from Beijing to the Caspian Sea and had raided Persia and Russia. These conquests were but the first stage of the Mongol Empire. Genghis Khan's successors would extend their power over the whole of China, Persia, and most of Russia.

CHAPTER 4

AN EMPIRE IN DECLINE

hile Genghis Khan was still living, he divided the Mongol Empire between four of his sons. Chagatai was given most of Turkistan and part of western China. Ögödei received western Mongolia and part of northwestern China. Genghis Khan's son Tolui received eastern Mongolia. The oldest son, Jöchi, received southwestern Siberia, western Turkistan, and Russian lands stretching north of the Black Sea. When Jöchi died in 1227, his lands in the west were inherited by his own son, Batu.

THE RISE OF ÖGÖDEI KHAN

After Ghenghis Khan's death, a convocation of Mongol leaders appointed Ögödei the next great khan. He immediately set out to conquer more of China. By 1234, all but the southern-most region of China had been added.

Genghis Khan and his wife Börte apportion parts of their empire to their four sons.

35

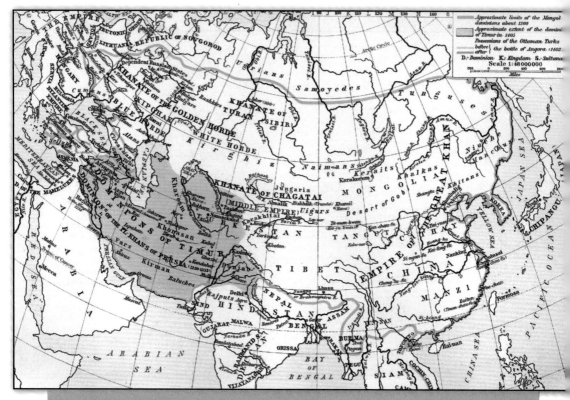

At its greatest extent the Golden Horde—the western part of the Mongol Empire—covered most of European Russia from the Urals to the Carpathian Mountains and extended east deep into Siberia.

In the western part of the Empire in Russia and Eastern Europe, called the Golden Horde, Batu began a series of campaigns. In 1240, Mongol forces laid siege to the city of Kiev. After days of bombarding the city via catapult, the walls came down and hand-to-hand combat began. Perhaps only 2,000 out of the city's 50,000 inhabitants were left alive. Resistance in Russia ceased. At its peak, the Golden Horde included most of European Russia from the Urals to the Carpathians, and it extended eastward deep into Siberia.

In 1241, Batu ordered Sübeedei to plan an invasion of Europe. Sübeedei sent two armies to

THE MONGOL POSTAL SYSTEM

The *yam* was a communications system likely developed during the reign of Genghis Khan and perfected under Ögödei. Venetian merchant and adventurer Marco Polo claimed that yam messengers carried communications up to 250 miles (400 kilometers) per day. Messages could be sent from one end of Mongol territory to the other, from Eastern Europe to the Sea of Japan. The yam operated under the army, who set up stations every few miles so that messengers could change horses and get supplies. The yam, basically an early kind of postal system, was an essential part of managing the empire and inspired similar systems in other cultures, including the Egyptians and Ottoman Turks.

In this nineteenth-century illustration, Marco Polo is welcomed into the court of Kublai Khan. Some of what we know about the Mongols comes from the Venetian trader's accounts.

Hungary and a third to Poland. He sought to prevent the forces of Europe from uniting. At the Battle of Legnica, the Mongols attacked the army of **Duke Henry II of Silesia** (a region now in southwestern Poland). Duke Henry had been planning to link his army to the army of Bohemia (in today's Czech Republic), but the Mongols met them first on April 9, 1241.

Duke Henry's troops were unnerved by the nearly silent Mongols. Employing flags as signals, the Mongols used several maneuvers to separate parts of the European army, including the feigned retreat, splitting the knights from the infantry. They then used a smoke screen to keep the forces apart while decimating each. Duke Henry was eventually killed, and his head placed on a spear.

In 1240, the army of Batu, grandson of Genghis Khan, sacked and burned Kiev, then the major city in Russia. Only the death of the supreme khan saved Europe from Batu's grip.

The Mongol victors counted the dead by removing each soldier's right ear, filling nine sacks in total.

Terrorizing Eastern Europe, Batu's armies reached central Germany before turning southward to establish themselves in Hungary. At the Battle of Mohi on April 11, 1241, the Mongols were nearly defeated by the Hungarians near the River Sajó. However, a force led by Sübeedei surprised the Hungarians by building a bridge across the river and attacking their rear flank, forcing them to retreat. The Mongol advance into Europe abruptly stopped in 1241 with the death of Ögödei Khan. Batu and his generals returned home for the election of a new supreme khan. The succession was disputed for several years.

THE YUAN DYNASTY: REIGN OF KUBLAI KHAN

Güyük, a son of Ögödei's widow, was elected great khan in 1246, but died two years later. He was succeeded by Möngke, a son of Tolui. Under him, the new conquests were in the Middle East. Hülegü, a brother of Möngke, conquered what are now Iran, Iraq, and Syria in the 1250s, resulting in the creation of a kingdom of nearly independent rulers, the Il-khans of Persia. In the east, the Mongols opened another campaign against China, during which Möngke died in 1279. He was succeeded by his brother Kublai.

Kublai Khan marked a turning point in Mongol history. He completed the conquest and unification of China, which had been divided under different rulers for a few hundred years.

39

In this portrait, Kublai Khan's Mongol identity is unmistakable because of his plain robe, leather hat, and braided hair.

To accomplish this, the Mongol army faced major obstacles. Their strength was always in their cavalry, and combat on horseback was difficult in South China's forests and agricultural lands. Their horses had little to eat, and the heat was intense. To capture the southeast coast, the Mongols had to develop a navy. However, during the final battle of the campaign in 1279, the Chinese emperor drowned. Kublai Khan established a new dynasty, called the Yuan (or Mongol) Dynasty.

FRAGMENTATION AND DISRUPTION

After Kublai Khan's death in 1294, the Mongol Empire fragmented. It was a demonstration of the strength of the Mongol army that the empire had lasted as long as it did. The Mongols had no developed concept for ruling settled populations. The various territories were placed under the authority of military commanders. Mongol khans relied on their subjects and on foreigners to administer their empire. Over time, power shifted from the Mongols to their officials, and this, added to the continual feuding among the different khanates, led to the empire's decline.

From 1300 on, disputes over succession and frequent rebellions weakened the central government in China. In 1368, the Mongols lost China to the native Ming dynasty. In the same period in the Middle East, the Il-khans lost power, and the western Golden Horde was defeated by a Muscovy-led alliance in 1380. Soon the empire was reduced to the Mongol homeland and scattered khanates. Eventually Ming invasions into Mongolia effectively ended Mongol unity.

The most enduring part of the Mongol Empire was the Golden Horde. It had begun to decline significantly in the 1340s, however, after outbreaks of the plague and the murder of one of its rulers. The Golden Horde broke apart

41

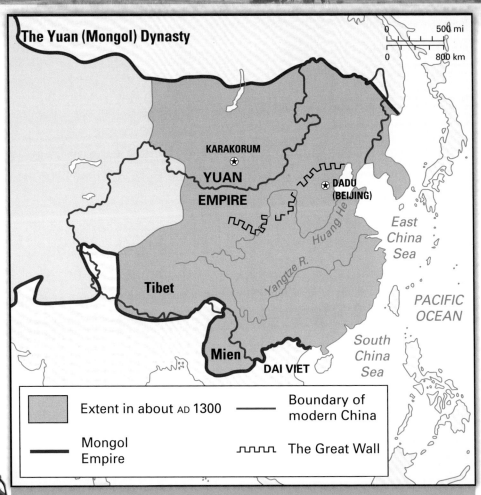

The Yuan (Mongol) Dynasty

KARAKORUM
★
YUAN
EMPIRE
★ DADU
(BEIJING)

East
China
Sea

Huang He

Tibet

Yangtze R.

PACIFIC
OCEAN

Mien

DAI VIET

South
China
Sea

	Extent in about AD 1300		Boundary of modern China
	Mongol Empire		The Great Wall

0   500 mi

0   800 km

The Yuan (Mongol) empire in China (c. 1300), showing the extent of its territory reached under Kublai Khan

into several smaller territories in the fifteenth century.

As guns and gunpowder replaced swords and bows and arrows as weapons, the skills of the Mongol warrior were no longer as effective. The Mongol people gradually assimilated among the many cultures they had once ruled, though some remained nomads on the steppe of Central Asia. However, the feats of the Mongol warrior and the empire they built remain a striking chapter in medieval history.

GLOSSARY

assimilate To fully become part of a different society, country, etc.

autonomous Having the power or right to govern oneself.

cavalry The part of an army that in the past had soldiers who rode horses.

consolidation The process of unifying.

convocation A large formal meeting.

dynasty A family of rulers who rule over a country for a long period of time. Also, the period of time when a particular dynasty is in power.

embellish To heighten by adding fanciful details.

feign To pretend.

infantry The part of an army that has soldiers who fight on foot.

javelin A long, light spear that people once threw as a weapon of war; today, it is thrown for distance as a sporting event.

lance A long, pointed weapon used in the past by knights riding on horses.

mace A heavy often spiked staff or club used especially in the Middle Ages for breaking armor.

maneuver A planned movement of soldiers. Also, to move in a planned way.

massacre To violently kill many people.

pastoral Relating to raising livestock.

plague A disease that causes death and that spreads quickly to a large number of people.

psychological Directed toward the will or toward the mind.

raid A surprise attack on an enemy by soldiers or other military forces. Also, to attack in a surprising way.

sack To plunder a town, especially after a capture.

siege A situation in which soldiers surround a city in order to try to take control of it.

steppe A large, flat area of land with grass and very few trees, especially in eastern Europe and Asia.

subordinate In a position of less power or authority than someone else.

tactics The science and art of disposing and maneuvering forces in combat.

tribute Money or goods that a ruler or country gives to another ruler or country, especially for protection.

FOR FURTHER READING

Adams, Simon. *Warrior: Sacrifice and Honour*. Dorking, Surrey, UK: Templar, 2011.

Bankston, John. *Genghis Khan*. Hockessin, DE: Mitchell Lane Publishers, 2014.

Dittmar, Brian. *Mongol Warriors*. Minneapolis, MN: Bellwether Media, 2012.

Hanson, Anders, and Elissa Mann. *Biggest, Baddest Book of Warriors*. Minneapolis, MN: ABDO Publishing, 2013.

Hyslop, Stephen G., and Patricia Daniels. *Great Empires: An Illustrated Atlas*. Washington, DC: National Geographic Society, 2011.

Medina, Nico. *Who Was Genghis Khan?* New York, NY: Grosset & Dunlap, 2014.

Pipe, Jim. *Wild Warriors*. Mankato, MN: Smart Apple Media, 2011.

Sepahban, Lois. *Mongol Warriors*. Mankato, MN: The Childs World Inc., 2015.

WEBSITES

Because of the changing nature of internet links, Rosen Publishing has developed an online list of websites related to the subject of this book. This site is updated regularly. Please use this link to access this list:

http://www.rosenlinks.com/WAW/mongol

INDEX